YOUR BODY BATTLES A COLD

WRITTEN BY **VICKI COBB** PHOTOMICROGRAPHS BY **DENNIS KUNKEL**
ILLUSTRATIONS BY **ANDREW N. HARRIS**

Ⅳ Millbrook Press / Minneapolis

NOTE: The photomicrographs in this book were taken with a scanning electron microscope (SEM). The photos are originally in black and white. A computer program is used to add color, often to highlight interesting features. The colors used do not show the real colors of the subject. The × followed by a number indicates magnification. For example, ×250 means the object in the picture is 250 times larger than its real size.

The author gratefully acknowledges the research assistance of Dr. Birgit Winther, assistant professor of otolaryngology, University of Virginia Health System. She is especially grateful for to Dr. Winther for working with Dennis Kunkel to create the micrographs on pages 13 and 17. Images of the rhinoviruses invading epithelial cells are a first for medicine. She also thanks Mary Slamin and Gail Fell, children's librarians from the Greenburgh, New York Public Library for assistance with the Further Reading list.

Dennis Kunkel would like to thank Delta Westcot for thin sectioning of nasal tissue for the rhinovirus/epithelial cells electron microscopy.

For Jillian Davis Cobb —VC

This series is dedicated to my mom, Carmen Kunkel, for the care she gives her children and grandchildren —DK

For William, Isabelle, and Kate who always have runny noses —ANH

Millbrook Press
A division of Lerner Publishing Group, Inc.
241 First Avenue North
Minneapolis, MN 55401 U.S.A.

Website address: www.lernerbooks.com

Library of Congress Cataloging-in-Publication Data

Cobb, Vicki.
    Your body battles a cold / by Vicki Cobb ; with photomicrographs by Dennis Kunkel ; illustrated by Andrew N. Harris.
        p.   cm. — (Body Battles)
    Includes bibliographical references and index.
    ISBN 978-0-8225-6813-1 (lib. bdg. : alk. paper)
    1. Cold (Disease)—Juvenile literature. I. Harris, Andrew, 1977– ill. II. Title.
RF361.C63 2009
616.2'05—dc22   2008002839

Manufactured in the United States of America
1 2 3 4 5 6 – DP – 14 13 12 11 10 09

Don't you just hate to get a cold? You sneeze a lot. Your nose drips. Your head feels stuffed. You don't feel like your usual peppy self. What a drag! A cold takes place at the back of your nose. It is like a battle going on in your body. And thanks to the superheroes of your body, it is a battle you will win! This book tells the story.

NEUTROPHIL

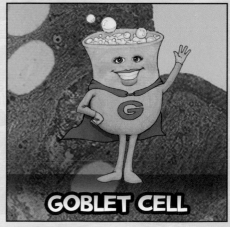

GOBLET CELL

PLASMA CELL

CILIA

Your whole body, including your nose, is made of very tiny living things called cells. Cells are so tiny that they can only be seen with a microscope—a powerful magnifying glass.

This is a white blood cell seen through a transmission electron microscope (TEM). A TEM can magnify a subject up to one million times. You can clearly see the grainy, brown and yellow nucleus (control center) of this cell.

4

You have many kinds of cells that do different jobs in your body.

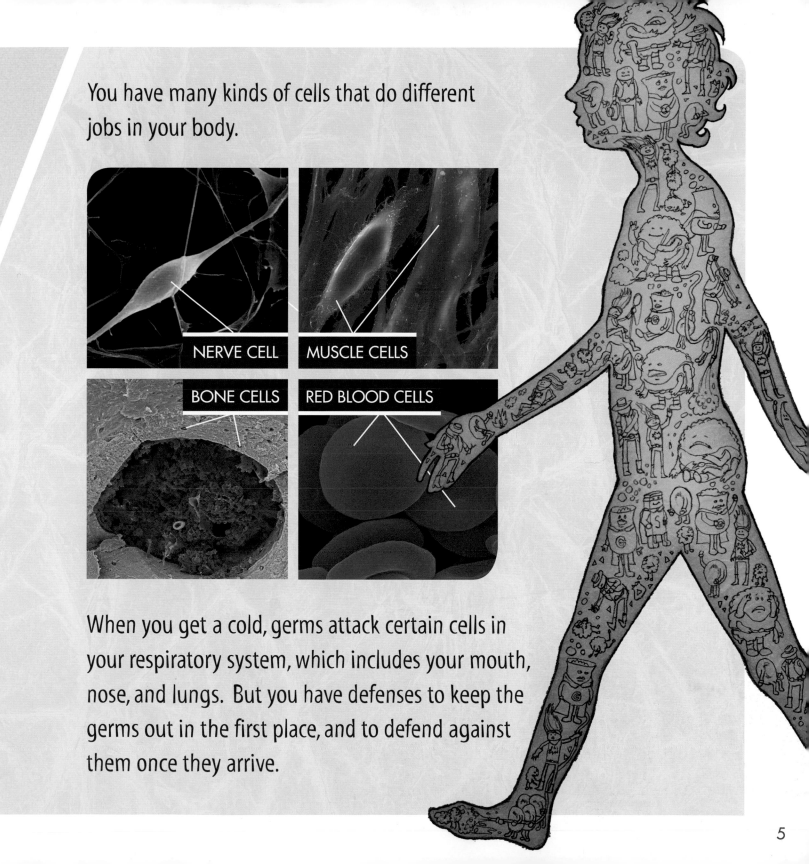

NERVE CELL

MUSCLE CELLS

BONE CELLS

RED BLOOD CELLS

When you get a cold, germs attack certain cells in your respiratory system, which includes your mouth, nose, and lungs. But you have defenses to keep the germs out in the first place, and to defend against them once they arrive.

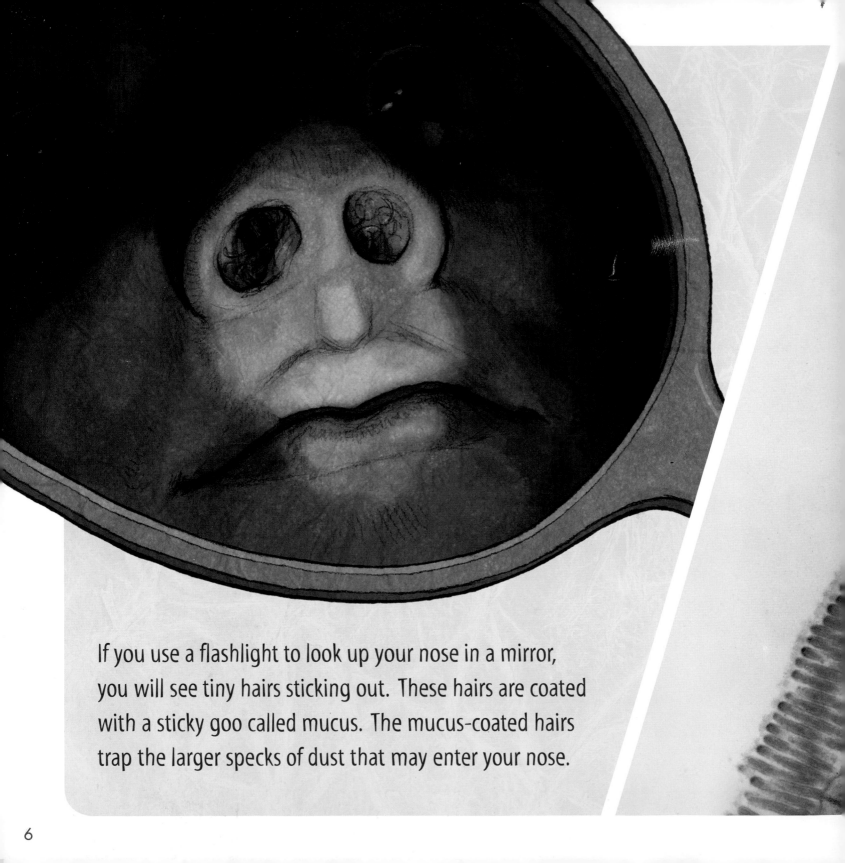

If you use a flashlight to look up your nose in a mirror, you will see tiny hairs sticking out. These hairs are coated with a sticky goo called mucus. The mucus-coated hairs trap the larger specks of dust that may enter your nose.

Mucus is formed in cup-shaped cells throughout the lining of the nose. They are called goblet cells not because they form gobs of goo (which they do) but because they often have stems like goblets. The nasal lining is covered with microvilli, hairlike "fingers" that increase the surface area for absorbing oxygen.

X18,475

MUCUS GLOBULE

MICROVILLI

NASAL LINING CELL

GOBLET CELL

X25,200   CILIA

To further protect you, some cells in your nose have microscopic hairs on them called cilia. (Just one is a cilium.) Cilia move back and forth in waves, brushing particles that don't belong in your nose down your throat. From there, the particles travel to your stomach, where digestive juices kill them. The nasal cells with cilia are the main targets for cold viruses.

When you don't have a cold, place a small mirror under your nose. Breathe out once. Look at the mirror. You will see two spots of cloudy moisture where the air from your nose hits the mirror. One spot is larger than the other. This nostril is doing most of the breathing. If you try this again in a few hours, the other nostril may make the bigger spot. It's amazing how your nostrils take turns and you never know it!

When you don't have a cold, air enters your body through your nose and goes down a windpipe to your lungs. Your nose does more than decorate the airholes in the middle of your face. It is built to do several jobs. The inside of your nose warms up the air as it enters your body. It also adds moisture to the air.

And it traps some of the tiny dirt particles and germs that enter your body with every breath you take. When you get a cold, the whole picture changes!

Most colds are caused by a germ called a rhinovirus. *Rhino* means "nose." A virus is a very small germ, smaller than most cells. You get a cold when a rhinovirus attacks the cells at the back of your nose.

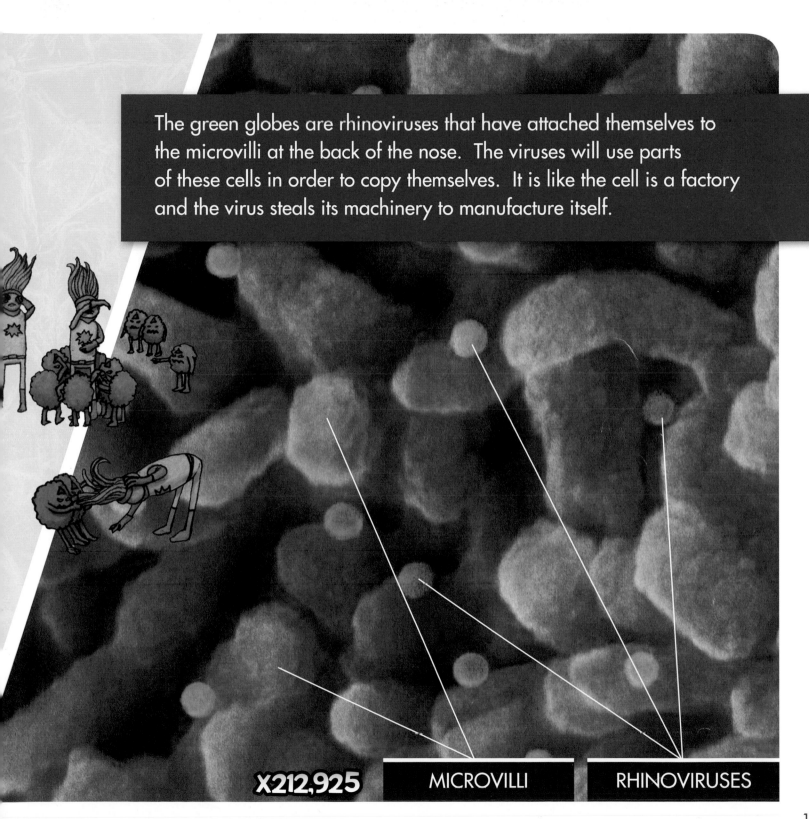

The green globes are rhinoviruses that have attached themselves to the microvilli at the back of the nose. The viruses will use parts of these cells in order to copy themselves. It is like the cell is a factory and the virus steals its machinery to manufacture itself.

X212,925

MICROVILLI

RHINOVIRUSES

Your nose doesn't take a rhinovirus attack lying down! Almost instantly, the invaded cells give off a kind of juice that acts like an alarm. The rest of your body springs into action. One of your first defenses is the sneeze. A muscle under your lungs pushes up, squeezing the air in your lungs into a much smaller space. This squeezed air is like the bubbles in a closed bottle of soda. Suddenly your air passages open and the sneeze explodes out of your mouth. The blast of air from a sneeze can be as fast as a hurricane's wind—100 miles (161 kilometers) an hour. A sneeze can contain five thousand droplets (with cold viruses in them) and travel up to 12 feet (3.7 meters). So cover your mouth when you sneeze!

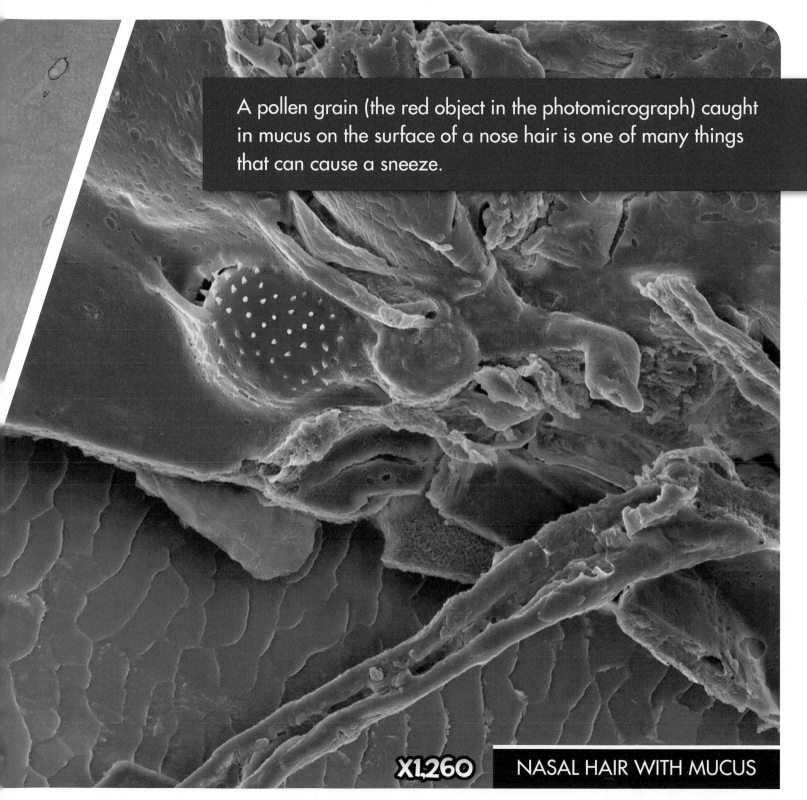

A pollen grain (the red object in the photomicrograph) caught in mucus on the surface of a nose hair is one of many things that can cause a sneeze.

X1,260   NASAL HAIR WITH MUCUS

Right after you sneeze, a group of cells in your nose, called goblet cells, produces watery mucus. When you get a cold, goblet cells make five to ten times more mucus then normal. Some of it just drips, but some gets brushed by the cilia cells to the back of your nose and you swallow it. The mucus helps flood out some of the viruses.

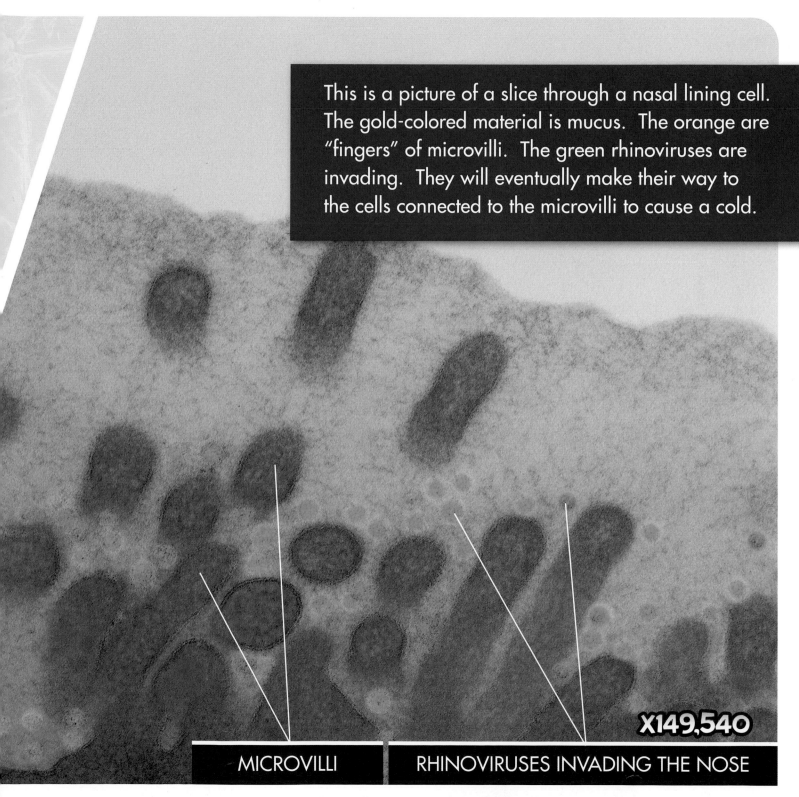

This is a picture of a slice through a nasal lining cell. The gold-colored material is mucus. The orange are "fingers" of microvilli. The green rhinoviruses are invading. They will eventually make their way to the cells connected to the microvilli to cause a cold.

X149,540

MICROVILLI

RHINOVIRUSES INVADING THE NOSE

Sneezing is also good because it blasts out germs and extra mucus. It helps keep your lungs and air passages from getting infected by the virus. A runny nose and sneezing tell you that your body is fighting back. You start this fight just after the virus enters your nose.

Blood, which includes red blood cells, virus-fighting white blood cells, and a lot of fluid, rushes to your nose to help. The inside of your nose swells up. It's hard to breathe through a stuffy nose. Fortunately, your nose and mouth are connected. So you now breathe through your mouth. But it's not as comfortable as breathing through your nose.

It takes a while to win the war. Your body needs about 10 days to make and use a special weapon that has only one job to do—namely, ruin every invading rhinovirus so that they can no longer attack your cells. The special weapon-making cells are in your blood. They are a kind of white blood cell called a plasma cell.

Plasma cells make antibodies, which recognize foreign invaders in your body. The antibodies mainly destroy the invaders. They are also able to tag them so that other cells will be able to find the invaders and destroy them.

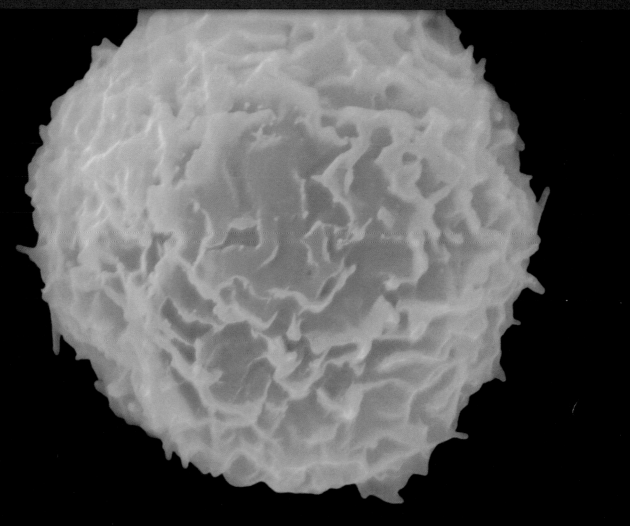

X19,600

PLASMA CELL

A plasma cell makes the perfect weapon to destroy the invading rhinovirus enemy. The surface of a rhinovirus has deep dents. It attaches to a cell by fitting a dent over a bump on the cell's surface, much like a plug into a socket. Plasma cells make a protein that fits exactly into the rhinovirus "socket." These proteins are called antibodies.

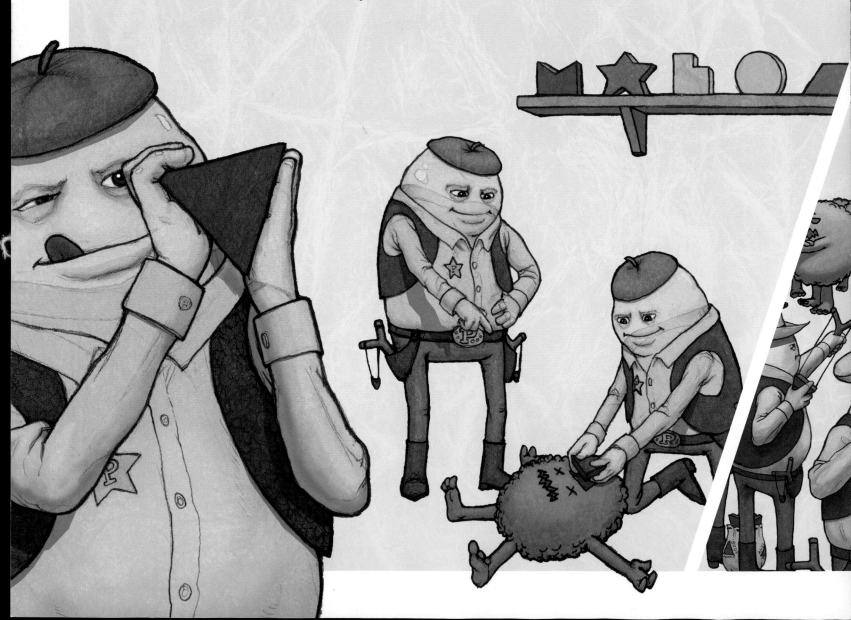

An antibody and a rhinovirus connect like two jigsaw puzzle pieces. The antibody plugs up the dent in an unattached virus where it would attach to your cells. Once that happens, the virus can't attach to a cell and it can no longer infect you.

A protein is a special kind of substance that makes up all living things. The word *protein* means "first importance." There are many different kinds of proteins. You eat foods that contain a lot of proteins such as meat, fish, eggs, and beans. These foods become part of the proteins of your body in your skin, muscles, and blood.

When your cold battle is over, dead cells and ruined viruses are all over the battlefield. Two types of white blood cells, neutrophils and macrophages, clean them up. The neutrophils and macrophages change shape to surround the virus.

Knobs grow out from the neutrophils and macrophages and wrap themselves around each side of a helpless virus. Suddenly the virus is inside the white cells. Powerful juices then digest it. When the neutrophils and macrophages are full, they also die. At the end of a cold, the mucus in your nose gets thick and yellowish because it contains a lot of dead white cells. It's a sign that you are almost all better.

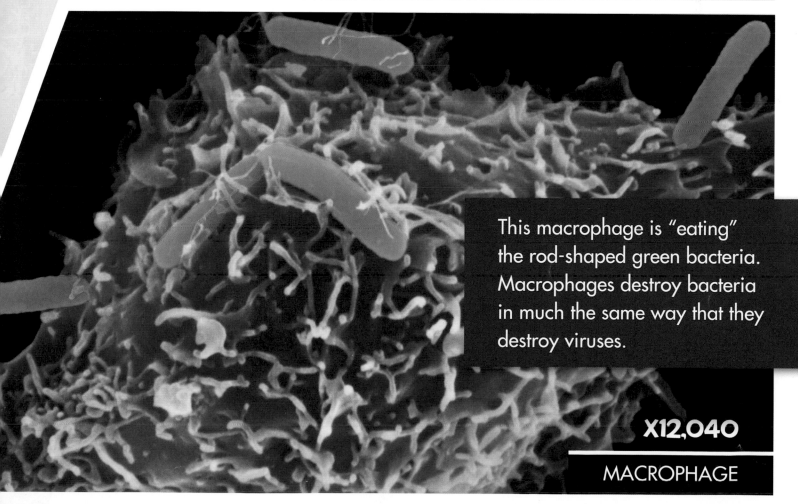

This macrophage is "eating" the rod-shaped green bacteria. Macrophages destroy bacteria in much the same way that they destroy viruses.

X12,040

MACROPHAGE

The good news is that you are now protected against the specific type of rhinovirus that gave you the cold. If this particular type of rhinovirus ever enters your body again, there are antibodies ready to take them out before they ever get started.

You will keep the antibodies you made in your blood for many years, perhaps the rest of your life. They are the prize for the battle your body has fought hard and won.

The bad news is that there are more than one hundred different kinds of rhinoviruses and you have protection only from those viruses that have already invaded you. But don't worry. Your body heroes are still there waiting to battle any new invaders.

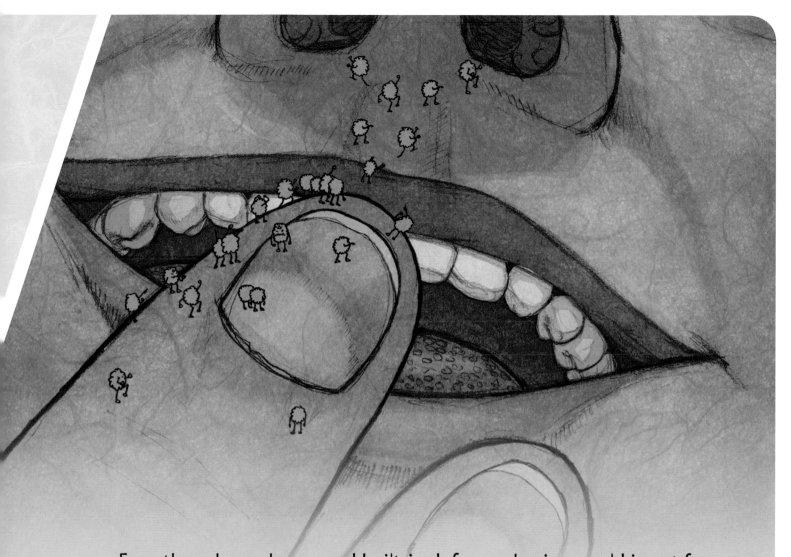

Even though you have good built-in defenses, having a cold is not fun. So do your best to keep from getting invaded in the first place. The most common way that rhinoviruses get into your body is by traveling from your hands into your eyes or nose or mouth. So wash your hands well and often. Then both you and your body heroes will have some well-earned peace.

GLOSSARY

antibodies: proteins made by white blood cells to react with specific foreign invaders to the body, such as viruses, making them harmless. Antibodies give you immunity.

cell: the smallest unit of all living things considered to be alive. The smallest organisms consist of only one cell. Human beings are made of many different kinds of cells.

cilia: hairlike structures projecting from some cells. In the nose, the waving motion of cilia help move dust and other undesirable material out of the nasal passages.

germs: one-celled organisms that cause disease, including bacteria and viruses

goblet cells: specialized cells that manufacture mucus. Some goblet cells are found among the nasal lining cells.

lungs: two organs located in the chest, responsible for providing the blood with oxygen and cleaning the blood of carbon dioxide

macrophage: a white blood cell that cleans up sick and infected areas by "eating" germs and dead cells

microscope: a powerful magnifier that allows us to look at cells. There are two main kinds of microscopes:

An **electron microscope** uses electrons and can magnify even smaller structures. There are two types of electron microscopes—scanning (SEM), which can magnify up to 500,000 times, and transmission (TEM), which can magnify up to 1 million times.

An **optical microscope** uses light and can magnify up to 1,500 times the actual size.

microvilli: hairlike extensions that allow nasal lining cells to absorb more oxygen by increasing surface area

molecules: the smallest part of a substance that has all the properties of that substance. Molecules are made up of atoms.

mucus: a gooey secretion of certain glands and cells that help lubricate the body. Mucus helps flush out material brought into the nose by incoming air.

mucus gland: a group of cells that secrete mucus

neutrophil: a white blood cell that helps fight viruses and bacteria by moving from the blood to the infected area

photomicrograph: a photograph taken with the help of a microscope

plasma cell: a white blood cell that manufactures antibodies

protein: any of a group of complicated molecules that form all the basic structures of living things

red blood cells: the cells in the blood responsible for carrying oxygen to all parts of the body. Their red color comes from iron in each cell.

respiratory system: a group of organs that delivers oxygen to your blood

rhinovirus: the virus that causes a cold. There are more than one hundred different kinds.

sneeze: a reflex that creates a powerful explosion of air from the lungs to get rid of irritating material in the nose

white blood cells: colorless cells floating in the blood that are important to the immune system and fighting disease

FURTHER READING

Durant, Penny Raife. *Sniffles, Sneezes, Hiccups, and Coughs.* New York: DK Publishing, 2005.

Hicks, Terry Allan. *The Common Cold.* Tarrytown, NY: Marshall Cavendish Benchmark, 2006.

Houghton, Gillian. *Breathe: The Respiratory System.* New York: PowerKids Press, 2007.

Jango-Cohen, Judith. *The Respiratory System.* Minneapolis: Lerner Publications Company, 2005.

Johnson, Rebecca L. *Daring Cell Defenders.* Minneapolis: Millbrook Press, 2008.

Mitchell, Melanie. *Killing Germs.* Minneapolis: Lerner Publications Company, 2006.

Parker, Steve. *Heart, Blood, Lungs.* Milwaukee: Gareth Stevens, 2005.

WEBSITES

Commoncold, Inc.
http://www.commoncold.org/special1.htm
This site discusses many of the myths that have built up around the common cold.
http://www.commoncold.org/undrstn2.htm
A list of basic facts about colds and insights on what to expect when a cold comes on are offered.

Common Cold Centre
http://www.cardiff.ac.uk/biosi/associates/cold/commoncold.html
A British site defines the common cold as well as discusses alternative treatments and summer colds.

KidsHealth
http://www.kidshealth.org/kid/ill_injure/sick/colds.html
This site has a discussion of the common cold with lots of cool information for kids.

INDEX